THE LIFE AND WISDOM OF
BENEDICT

THE 'SAINTS ALIVE' SERIES

THE LIFE AND WISDOM OF
BENEDICT

Written and Compiled by
LAVINIA BYRNE

ALBA·HOUSE   NEW·YORK

SOCIETY OF ST. PAUL, 2187 VICTORY BLVD., STATEN ISLAND, NEW YORK 10314

British Library Cataloguing in Publication Data:
A record for this book is available from the British Library.

ISBN 08189 08688

Typeset in Monotype Columbus by
Strathmore Publishing Services, London N7.

Printed and bound in Great Britain by
Mackays of Chatham PLC, Chatham, Kent.

Hodder and Stoughton Ltd,
A division of Hodder Headline PLC,
338 Euston Road, London NW1 3BH

CONTENTS

INTRODUCTION

———◆———

Who are the saints and why should we bother to
know about their lives? We are inclined to think
of them as heroic people who did extraordinary
things, or as people who suffered a great deal
and were somehow specially gifted or good.
What we then forget is that, in general, saints are
people like us. They struggled to know themselves better, to be more kind and loving, more
self-accepting, less neurotic. They did not always
succeed. They thought their attempts to live with
integrity would make them closer to other people and to God. Often what they then discovered
was that other people became harder to love and
that God simply disappeared.

Yet they kept up the struggle. They believed
that they were given one chance, that they had to
live with a certain generosity, because this life is
a preparation for the full glory of the next life.
They then learnt that we are given many chances

because all is grace, and the Christian life is a life of grace. So their schemes and plans for being holy were dismantled. All that was asked of them was a readiness to accept the gifts of God, including the final gift of heaven.

Saints come from every walk of life. They are men and women who share our concerns about money, power, politics, peace, energy, food, war, death, sex, love, privacy, the inner life, the outer life, harmony, balance. What makes them distinctive is that they looked beyond themselves to know how best to live and they discovered that God shared their concerns. If we read about them nowadays, we do so out of more than simple curiosity. Their lives are worth reading because we can learn from them. We look for more than a good example, though. The saints seem to know more than we do; they have access to a deeper level of wisdom than our own. They are gurus for our times. So when we read about them, we are quite right to seek an insight into the mind of God, who calls and inspires us all to the heroism of holiness, however we ourselves happen to live. Holiness is for all, not just the few; for a holy life is no more than a life lived in the presence of God.

In our materialistic and agnostic age, do the saints still matter? Have they any wisdom for us, or are they simply a pious irrelevance? Are their lives mere legends or do they have some significance beyond the bare bones of what history tells us about them?

Benedict was the father of Western monasticism. He was the first person to try to understand how we can live together with any degree of authenticity. He laid out systems for leadership, ownership and belonging; for formation, training and shared living. He was concerned to understand how moderation and balance can influence the way in which we live. He examined the responsibilities of leaders, and the duties of those whom they serve. His ideas are relevant for the Church nowadays, but are also – and quite exceptionally – relevant for the world of politics and even of European unity.

Benedict was a monk and a layman. He was a scholar and a saint. Benedictine monks brought an alternative system into the world.

They cultivated the desert and the wilderness, they tamed the wild. In time, their monasteries became powerhouses of scholarship and learning. How can this help us nowadays? What can we learn from the *Rule of St Benedict*, the greatest document of the Western Church?

PART ONE

The Story of His Early Years

'Listen, turn the ear of thine heart'

PART ONE

───────◆───────

'Listen, turn the ear of thine heart'

Benedict's early years

'Listen.' The first word of the Rule of St Benedict invites us to a conversation. The Abbot asks us to listen to his words and to the call of God. We can hear and we can speak; God addresses us and we answer. God calls us to action, to take stock of ourselves, and offers us the fruits of a life of obedience. But there is no sense of undue haste, of a crippling immediacy which might reduce us to a frenzy. Conversation with God is desirable, but it takes time because it takes place within time. It is embodied and it requires us to be embodied, as part of the community of the body of Christ.

Listen. Listen to yourself and listen to God. Listen also to Benedict. Who was this man and why has his influence on the culture of the West been so great? He was born in Nursia in AD 480, seventy years after Alaric the Goth had laid waste to Rome. His biographer, Pope Gregory the Great, explains to us that his was a Christian world. The pagan world of the Roman Empire was a vanishing memory. East and West were cut off from each other by the barbarian invaders, however, and came to understand less and less about each other's Christianity. If people visited Rome, it was on pilgrimage to look for the tomb of St Peter, or to venerate the saints. Churches there were named after Saints John and Paul, Stephen and Lawrence, Agnes, Cecilia, Sabina and Clement. Instead of the temples of the ancient world, huge new basilicas rose in their place, dedicated to Saints Peter and Paul and, at the Lateran, to John the Baptist.

Out in the Sabine countryside, in the walled city of Nursia, Benedict was protected from the conflict which pitted the Goths against the people of Britain, Gaul, Italy and North Africa. The days of empire were over. In Italy power lay in the hands of Odoacer the Visigoth. Yet he died at the hand of a new invader when Benedict was nine: Theodoric, King of the Ostrogoths, occupied the country in 489 and took possession of

Rome. He chose to build his palace at Ravenna, adorning it with rich mosaics. Though technically a heretic, being an Arian Christian, Theodoric was a good ruler. In 496 Clovis, the King of France, converted to Christianity and Gaul now provided a focus for orthodoxy. The stage was being set for further hostile conflict, but also for the dawn of a new age; a dark age, but one of great promise.

As a young man Benedict moved to Rome to pursue his studies. Pope Gregory the Great, his biographer, tells us almost nothing about his childhood. All we know is that the boy came from a well-to-do family and that he had a sister called Scholastica. A contemporary wrote of the city of Rome where Benedict came to live: 'The ancients counted seven wonders of the world, but all of them are thrown into the shade by the astonishing spectacle presented by this city: it can be said in truth that the whole of Rome is one great wonder.' The Coliseum was still in use; the Via Appia was the main highway; imperial fountains and aqueducts adorned the landscape. The conquering Goths had carried off the plate and silver, but they had left the buildings relatively intact. To a country boy, it must have looked glamorous in the extreme.

Rome was a Christian city. The reigning Pope was Gelasius I (492–6) when Benedict arrived there. Known principally for his liturgical reforms, Gelasius ensured that a common prayer book and set forms of services were followed. On his death a quiet man called Anastasius II succeeded to the papacy. Unfortunately he lasted only two years and then an undignified dispute broke out which must have influenced Benedict's thinking, for it demonstrated what happens when a community is divided and falls apart. There was a double papal election in 498. Most people voted for a deacon called Symmachus to become Pope and his candidacy was supported by Italy's ruler, Theodoric. The opposition favoured a man called Laurentius, an archpriest or senior presbyter who was consecrated at St Mary Major's. In 505 Theodoric took action. He had Laurentius banned from the city and supported Symmachus until the Pope's death in 514.

The dawn of his monastic vocation

There was another thread to Church life at the time and this began to exercise a deep fascination for Benedict. Monasticism was the order of the day. A custom which had originated in the deserts of the Eastern Church, the life of seclusion and withdrawal had spread into the Church of the West, largely through the influence of the Rule of Pachomius, the 'first monk'. In common with St Basil and John Cassian, he wrote down directives to guide his fellow monks and their subsequent followers. These 'rules' from the Church of the East reflected a way of life which had been developed in the wilderness. Many of the practices were extremely austere and better adapted to a warmer climate than that of Italy. If they kept the rule properly, the monks in the West suffered a great deal. So hard was it that many monks ended up tinkering with their rules and dodging their full force. When Benedict himself decided to adopt a life of seclusion, he did not join one of the Roman monasteries, as he considered them too worldly. Instead he set off into the country-side and at Affile, east of Rome, he began to live the life of a monk. Benedict had a companion with him at this time: his former nursemaid came with him into exile.

A legend is told which relates to this part of his life. It is one of the collection of miracle stories which Gregory included in his biography of Benedict. Contemporary historians are embarrassed by these legends as they do not carry the force of accurate historical information. Yet they were written within living memory of Benedict's death, so they must bear a grain of truth about the personality of the man. At Affile, so legend goes, his nurse had an accident with an earthenware sieve, breaking it clean in half. She was worried out of her mind and wept bitterly. Benedict came along to find out what the problem was, took the sieve from her, held its broken edges together and prayed over it. Not only did it mend perfectly, but Benedict's reputation began to spread. It was time to escape to the hills, making a clean break with his past.

The cave at Subiaco

Leaving his nurse behind, young Benedict set off

again, in search of true solitude. He went to Subiaco, five miles north of Affile, forty miles from Rome. Here he found a cave and the silence and space he craved, and also a spiritual guide – a monk called Romanus. Romanus took him bread, which he lowered on a rope to the young man, and offered him counsel and advice. It could be that he also lent Benedict books, for certainly it was at this stage in his development that Benedict began to read the Church Fathers as well as the Scriptures. His ideas about monasticism were being formed in the solitude of his cell and through his exposure to tales of the early Christian saints. He would later write that hermits 'must not let themselves be drawn away into the desert by the fervour of an overnight conversation, but they must learn to fight the devil after a long probation in the monastery; then, instructed by others as to these desert fights, they may, without help or consolation, but with the help of God, fight alone against the vice of the flesh and against evil thoughts'.

The course he was engaged on was a lonely one, and not to be undertaken lightly. Temptation stories abound in the lives of the early desert Fathers, and Gregory attributes a graphic one to the young Benedict. One day he was joined in his cell by a blackbird which flew around him, brushing his cheek with its wing. He could have caught it in his bare hand. At that moment he was assaulted by the memory of a woman he had once seen. 'The vice of the flesh and evil thoughts' threatened him, but rescue came when he plunged out of his cell into the undergrowth and threw himself onto the thorns of a rose bush.

Benedict lived alone for three years in the *sacro speco,* or cave, at Subiaco. During this period he developed the ideas which lie at the heart of the Rule. His sensitivity to the conversation with God which must take over the mind and heart of every monk became absolute. In silence and in solitude he learnt the meaning of the command he would later issue to those who would follow him. He learnt the value of the word 'listen'.

The first followers

Benedict's reputation for holiness began to grow. Near his cave at Subiaco there was a ruined villa, a summer palace which the Emperor Nero had constructed. He had also had the waters of the river Anio diverted by a system of dams, to provide himself with a lake. Hence the name Sublacum – meaning 'under the lake' – from which Subiaco is derived. The stones from this villa provided building materials for the men who now came to join Benedict, and they constructed small huts to live in. Over the remaining years which he spent at Subiaco the movement grew fast. Soon there were twelve independent little monasteries, each with twelve monks and an abbot. Benedict trained those who came to join and accepted overall charge for the group. This was the modest beginning of the great civilising force we call Benedictine monasticism.

This modesty makes even more bizarre the fact that Gregory's account of these years is illustrated with miracles that read like ancient fairy stories. Is this all there is to remember of those early years? There is a playfulness about these stories which destroys our preconceptions about how the religious life ought to be. Three of the twelve monasteries were built high up on the cliff face, with no water supply. The monks came down to tell Benedict of the problem they had shifting buckets from Nero's artificial lake to their huts. That night, Benedict went up the mountain and prayed there. He took with him a child, Placidus, who had been confided to his care by the boy's father, a man called Tertullus. With Placidus watching, Benedict took three stones and put them on the ground. The following day he sent for the monks from the three monasteries. 'Go and dig into the ground at that place, for Almighty God can cause water to spring forth from the summit of a mountain, and thus you will be dispensed from your painful journey to go and get it.' They duly dug, and the water still runs out of the ground there to this day.

The next miracle is also concerned with water. Placidus went to the lake with a pitcher to collect fresh water. He lost his balance and fell in, the current pulled him away from the shore and he was in desperate danger. Benedict was indoors at the time, saying his prayers. He had a premonition of danger and sent for another monk, called Maurus. 'Brother Maurus, run quickly, the child has fallen into the lake and the current is carrying him away,' he said. Maurus ran out, got to Placidus, yanked him to safety by his hair and dragged him to the shore. It was only then that he took stock and realised that he had been walking on the water of the lake. Benedict attributed this feat to his disciple's spirit of obedience. He had done what he was told. Maurus demurred and attributed the miracle to Benedict. Little Placidus resolved the argument by saying, 'When they pulled me out of the water I saw over my head Father Abbot's mantle, and I felt it was he who was saving me.'

Benedict himself was soon in danger, for a local priest called Florentius was jealous of his influence and wanted to kill him. He sent a poisonous loaf of bread to Benedict who took one look at it and commanded a raven to carry it away and hide it in a place where it could not harm anyone. The bird flew off with the poisonous bread in its mouth, dumped it and subsequently returned daily to Benedict for its food. Another miracle story from Gregory the Great's collection. Another story with biblical resonances, this time drawn from the life of the prophet Elijah, who was also visited by a raven and received safe bread from God.

Benedict's saving mantle was now poised to cover a far greater community than that gathered at Subiaco. There were other souls who needed the nourishment of those wells within the human spirit which he alone knew how to tap. The time had come to leave Subiaco and to set out for the wider world. His little troop of followers took a fortnight to walk due south to Monte Cassino, a mountain in the Apennines. The year was 530 and Benedict was in his prime. The monks' journey took them down the Via Latina, the road from Rome to Naples, as they marched in the footsteps of the legionaries. At the top of Monte Cassino was a former acropolis where the Roman legions had once camped. It too provided building materials for the new construction which Benedict now planned. Apart from the vestiges of army occupation, there were other historical markers also. Jupiter had most likely been worshipped on this mountain. Certainly there was a statue of Apollo there, and a sacred grove.

Benedict had a field day. The ancient temple was dedicated to St Martin, and an oratory was built to St John the Baptist. The sacred grove became the monastery garden. But in his *Dialogues,* where he gives us an early account of the foundation at Monte Cassino, Gregory the Great tells us that the old and the new warred on each other. Indeed, pagan spirits came out to attack the incomers. Voices were heard in the grounds crying out, '*Maledictus*, not *Benedictus*, accursed not blessed!' making a play on the saint's name. A monk found an idol in the grounds and took it into the kitchen by mistake. It went off like an incendiary bomb, blinding the cooks. Benedict was drawn to the place by the sound of distressed monks, had them sign themselves with the sign of the cross, and the evil spirit withdrew. A child who was helping with the construction of a wall was crushed by stones rained down on him by the evil spirits. They brought his corpse to Benedict in a sack. He prayed over the child's body, the boy was restored to life, and went straight back to get on with building the wall. These are stories about a project undertaken in the name of God, about the triumph of good over evil, about new life and the restoration of hope where there was none.

Life in the monastery of Monte Cassino
With the completion of the buildings and the arrival of a score of recruits, all of whom Benedict undertook to train, life could fall once more into natural patterns and routines. We get a snapshot of what the place looked like from an account in the Rule: 'It is to be desired that the monastery contain all that is necessary for life; water, a mill, a garden, a kneading-trough, and that the various trades are exercised within the monastery walls, that the monks are dispensed from the necessity of going far away, which harms their souls.' This is a place where every need will be met, where the very structure of the entire enterprise is intended to serve the needs of the brethren, where they can live an ordered life of service, praising and loving God. It is also a place of hard work and scholarship, an unsentimental place where there is great work to be done in the Lord's service.

Benedict thought long and hard about its design. He himself had already tried out several versions of the monastic life. From his Rome days he recalled the insights of Gelasius about the need for well-organised liturgy. From the memory of the Church's decline under warring candidates for the papacy, he learnt the importance of due processes and of the good exercise of authority. Anarchy and chaos do no one any good at all, whereas a well-ordered way of life serves the deepest needs of the brethren. The experience of withdrawal from the world at Affile and then of solitude at Subiaco had taught him about the importance of silence, the place of that conversation with God which is initiated by the divine command to us that we should listen. From the time of expansion at Subiaco he recalled the value of simplicity, a way of life in which small groups live in harmony but also with a degree of autonomy from each other. Here at Monte Cassino he initiated something new again. The accumulated experiences of his past life gave him the authority to go for something grandiose in its design yet simple in its execution. Here was to be nothing less than a 'school of the Lord's service'.

The grand design
The Prologue to the Rule of St Benedict sets out his purpose:

> Listen, my son, and turn the ear of thine heart to the precepts of thy Master. Receive readily, and faithfully carry out the advice of a loving Father, so that by the work of obedience you may return to Him, whom you have left by the sloth of disobedience. For thee, therefore, whosoever thou be, my words are intended, who, giving up thy own will, dost take the all-powerful and excellent arms of obedience to fight under the Lord Christ, the true King.
>
> First, beg of Him with most earnest prayer to finish the good work begun; that He who now hath deigned to count us among His children may never be grieved by our evil deeds. For at all times we must so serve Him with the good things He has given us, that He may not, as an angry Father, disinherit His children, nor

as a dread Lord, provoked by our evil deeds,
deliver us to everlasting punishment as wicked
servants who refuse to follow Him to glory.

These words speak of a variety of relations —
those the individual monk has with Benedict;
those each of us has with God. God is portrayed
as a loving father, as the one who provides us
with good things. We serve God by taking up the
arms of obedience in order to fight in the service
of the Lord Christ, the true king. The enemy is
disobedience, which leads us away from the harmony and glory which God intends for us. How
are we to regain these? By entering into God's
service, submitting our will to his, allowing ourselves to be led by him and educated by him
throughout our lives. The image of a school of
the Lord's service is a dynamic one; what
Benedict envisages is that we should grow in
God's service:

We are therefore now about to institute a school
for the service of God in which we hope nothing harsh nor burdensome will be ordained. But

if we proceed in certain things with some little severity, sound reason so advising for the amendment of vices or the preserving of charity, do not for fear of this forthwith flee from the way of salvation, which is always narrow in the beginning. In living our life, however, and by the growth of faith, when the heart has been enlarged, the path of God's commandments is run with unspeakable loving sweetness; so that never leaving His school, but persevering in the monastery until death in His teaching, we share by our patience in the sufferings of Christ, and so merit to be partakers of His kingdom.

The promise is that 'nothing harsh or burdensome will be ordained'. Benedict speaks with unique authority, for his entire purpose is to build up the followers of Christ into a community of grace. If there are austerities, these come from the discipline of an organised and ordered way of life. They are not intended to be imposed as punishments. Benedict offers the monk a system for Christian living, not a series of hoops which we have to negotiate at our peril.

Benedict the monk

Benedict's sister Scholastica came to live in the desert too. She followed him to Monte Cassino and lived in a nearby village called Palombariola. They would meet once a year, on a specially designated day, to pray and enjoy talking to each other about God and the concerns of their respective communities. One year – we are not told the date – they met as usual, with some of the other monks present. As the day came to an end and they were having supper together, Scholastica asked Benedict not to leave the meeting place. She had a premonition that she was about to die. He could see no reason for not returning to the monastery and said so, intending to set off home. Scholastica put her head on the table and began to pray. Thunder and lightning promptly filled the night sky and Benedict was outwitted. He had to stay and go on talking to his sister. Three days later, sitting in his cell back at the monastery, Benedict saw his sister's soul winging its way past his window in the form of a dove, heaven-bound. He sent for her body, for she had indeed died, and had it buried in the tomb which was already set aside for his own death. Later he too would be buried in it, so that they were united in death.

Other visitors to the monastery had rather less difficulty gaining access to it, for civil war now afflicted Italy and this created a refugee population as whole villages were attacked by warring troops. Famine struck Campagna in 538 and people turned to the monks for help. The stories of Benedict's miracles at this time abound. He filled empty barrels with oil and created bread where there was none. Wherever there was need, he intervened. To these pious legends we can add the plain facts of what he actually wrote about his perceptions. He makes an important case for the duty of hospitality in the Rule:

> Above all let the abbot not fail to have a greater
> care for the souls of those confided to him than
> for the things which are terrestrial, temporal,
> and perishing, for he must render an account for
> those souls. And let him not be uneasy at the
> smallness of his resources, remembering what is
> written: 'Seek ye first the kingdom of God and

his justice, and the rest shall be added unto you.' And again, 'Nothing is wanting to those who fear him'.

The abbot's task was one of faith as well as hospitality.

There were other tasks which belonged to the ministry of good government which Benedict had now embraced. The abbot is appointed for life. Benedict committed himself to the service of his monks with no reservations. Other rulers and warlords rampaged around the countryside claiming vast tracts of land for themselves. Benedict meanwhile served God from the security of the monastery. Not only did he write the Rule but he also devised and revised a system of prayer which marks the Western Church to this day: in 575, nearly thirty years after Benedict's death, Gregory founded the monastery of St Andrew in the heart of Rome, where the monks lived by Benedict's Rule; in 596 Gregory sent Augustine to Canterbury to win souls for God in England. Again, they came bearing the Rule – and with it the Divine Office, the method of prayer which Benedict placed at its heart. We hear distant echoes of that heartbeat in the recitation of Matins, Evensong, or the Daily Prayer of the Church.

This sane and balanced way of praying together promised more than access to God. It would form the praying heart of those who used it. Whereas in Eastern monasticism the Book of Psalms had become a kind of mantra that monks had to repeat in its entirety every single day, now the Church had a simpler way of using them for reflective prayer. The whole book would be recited, but over the period of one week rather than one day. Rather than barraging God with sound, there was now the possibility of enjoying silence, the space between the words when God speaks to us, when we may truly listen.

Benedict, the praying monk and governor of souls, died in 547, not long after his sister. He had himself taken to the chapel of St John and stood there praying as his strength left him. He knew before he died that his great work at Monte Cassino would be destroyed, predicting its fall before he went. This destruction happened in

577, when the Lombards came out of Hungary and laid Italy waste. Monte Cassino was not spared. The monks just about escaped with their lives, taking the hand-written copy of the Rule into exile with them. Benedict was dead, and his monastry ruined, but the way of life would go on, a greater monument to Benedict's genius than any tomb could ever be.

PART TWO

The Wisdom of Benedict

'Let Christ be the chain that binds you'

PART TWO

'Let Christ be the chain that binds you'

The Rule of St Benedict

Some fifty years after Benedict's death, Gregory began to write about his life. Gregory was a monk, and in 590 he became the first monk in the Church's history to be made Pope. The living legacy of Benedict's achievements lies in the saintly men and women who live by the vision which inspired him. They can do this because he wrote the Rule, for those who came after him to follow. This is where we discover his gifts most dramatically at work. As Gregory said of it, 'Amongst all the wonders which draw a shining halo around Benedict even in this world, we must count the splendour of his doctrine; for he has written a Rule for monks which is conspicuous by reason of its moderation and the clarity of its language.' A later commentator, Abbot Gasquet, wrote, 'As a code of laws it has undoubtedly influenced Europe; and indeed

there is no other book, save of course the Holy
Bible, which with such certainty can be claimed
as a chief factor in the work of European civili-
sation.'

So what is it that makes the Rule great? How
does the wisdom of Benedict which is distilled
there, speak with an eloquent message for contemporary Europe – and the wider world? It is a
model document because of the moderation and
sanity with which it is written. It describes a way
of life by speaking directly to the people who are
to live it. It exhorts, encourages and consoles by
turns. Above all, it tells us to 'listen', to hearken
to its message and to the word of God.

'Let Christ be the chain that binds you.' The
stories about Benedict gained a certain intensity
during the years he spent with the community at
Monte Cassino. This quotation belongs to a tale
about a man called Martin. He had tied himself
to the wall of a cave near the monastery with a
metal chain. Benedict upbraided him, saying,
'Let Christ be the chain that binds you.'

Benedict witnessed and made possible an
important change to the history of human

asceticism. Whereas the earliest monks had gone out into the wilderness and sought a heroic form of life, punishing themselves into submission to the love of God, Benedict came to see things differently. Pachomius, Basil of Caesarea and John Cassian had paved the way. From an extreme, even abusive form of martyrdom, based on exceptional gifts and the emergence of charismatic leaders, they moved the Church on.

Benedict now developed the logic of their thinking. The life of faith is for the many, not the few. Martyrdom – the saintly opportunity offered by the experience of the early Church – had been reserved for special people, for those who could climb up Jacob's ladder and go heavenwards, bearing the scars of heroic conflict and victory. In contrast, Benedict's Rule offers a way of life based on obedience to God's will, to simplicity and humility. The way up is not through ascent, but through descent into obedience and self-knowledge. If Christ is the chain that binds us, then participation in Christ means participation in the common life. If the abbot is singled out in Benedict's scheme of things, this is because 'in the monastery, he is considered to take the place of Christ'. He is asked to be a man of God and also a good manager, not an exceptional, charismatic person. This is why we may trust him.

The abbot

The Rule begins with a description of the ministry of the abbot as leader of the community. On the one hand, 'an abbot to be fit to rule a monastery should ever remember what he is called, and in his acts illustrate his high calling'; and on the other, 'he should neither teach, ordain, nor require anything against the command of our Lord (God forbid!), but in the minds of his disciples let his orders and teaching be mingled with the leaven of divine justice'. With this simple formula, Benedict reveals his genius: the greater the power held by one man, the more it should be balanced by submission to God's overarching purpose for us all. The abbot is not to be an autocrat, or a dictator, or a wishy-washy fatherly type. He is to teach, ordain and require of people the same discipline to which he himself is subject, namely a thorough love of obedience.

He is to teach by example: 'He should first show the monks in deeds rather than words all that is good and holy.' He is to treat everyone well: 'Let him make no distinction of persons in the monastery. Let not one be loved more than another, save such as are found to excel in their good works. Let not the free-born be put before the serf-born in religion, unless there be other reasonable cause for it.' The abbot is not outside or above the system; he is one of the community, elected by the brethren to serve them for life. That is why Benedict uses community discernment when seeking the will of God. If something important has to be done or decided, the abbot is to call all the monks together, including the youngest – 'because the Lord often reveals to a younger member what is best'. If something less momentous is planned, 'let the abbot take advice of the seniors only'. The management practice laid out here would be baffling to many present-day entrepreneurs, who are inclined to deal only with their peers and to screen out the ideas and insights of younger or lesser members of the group, consulting them only rarely and usually just about trivial things.

The monks, however, form a community, an extended family, rather than a workforce. Benedict's wisdom is directed towards obedience to the will of God and a fruitful experience of the common life, rather than productivity and profitability. Yet many a workforce could benefit from the humanity he displays in the Rule, and many families would do well to reflect on it.

Monastic spirituality

What is the source of this humanity? Benedict lays it out for us in a chapter of the Rule entitled 'The instruments of good works'. He lists the 'tools of our spiritual craft' and insists that 'the workshop where all these instruments are made use of is the cloister of the monastery'. This is the language of art and creativity; the workshop is the place where the soul is hewn into shape, moulded to the will of God. It should come as no surprise, then, that the tools he lists are very functional and straightforward.

This is spirituality for everyone, not an esoteric mysticism for the few. It is deeply scriptural, with the Ten Commandments and the corporal and spiritual works of mercy at its heart.

Everyone in the monastery is bound by the same discipline. There are different categories of people there and Benedict has different chapters of the Rule for each: the abbot, the monks, children and old men, the sick, visitors, the novices and craftsmen or artificers. They are listed again, by function this time, with chapters on the prior, the senior monks, the cellarer, doorkeeper, the weekly cooks, those who read at table, and the master of novices. Yet whatever their office within the community, all are subject to the same fundamental disciplines. 'The mode of a monk's life ought at all times to favour that of Lenten observance,' Benedict writes. Now what does this mean?

The Rule sets out a way of life which can be observed. It is do-able because it offers practical guidelines about real things like food and clothing, how the monastery buildings are to be ordered – with separate cells for the sick, for instance — about the arrangement of time and about journeys. This is a spirituality which works from the outside inwards. By observing the Rule with all the fervour with which the Church keeps Lent, our inward attitudes become transformed. That is why the bulk of the text of the Rule is dedicated to practicalities, even while Benedict makes it quite clear, by placing his chapters on the virtues to which all should aspire at the beginning of the Rule, that the ultimate goal is the conversion of the heart which follows any conversion of manners.

The monastic virtues

Benedict learnt about the religious life in the solitude of his cave at Subiaco. Is this why he writes with such authority about obedience, silence and humility, and then about poverty and work? These are 'cave virtues', the virtues of survival. Obedience to God's will is at the centre of his entire enterprise. It is the key attitude he seeks to instil in his followers, whatever their circumstances.

So how are we to learn obedience? The cluster

of ideas represented by the active practice of silence, humility, poverty and work are integral to understanding Benedict's wisdom. For in silence we will hear God speaking to us. 'Because of the importance of silence, therefore, let leave to speak be seldom given, even to perfect disciples, although their talk be of good and holy matters and tending to edification, since it is written, "In much speaking, thou shalt not escape sin".' This is a severe discipline, because it requires us to cut out surplus and extraneous noise: the sounds we use to blank out our truest feelings, the sounds which protect us from the essential loneliness of the human condition. In the silence God can speak – and we can listen. The root meaning of the word 'obedience' is about listening. That is why silence has an absolute value in the life of the monk.

So, too, does humility, another Christ-like virtue. There are twelve steps to humility, according to Benedict:

When all these steps of humility have been mounted, the monk will presently attain to that love for God which is perfect and casteth out fear.

By means of this love everything which before he
had observed not without fear, he shall now
begin to do by habit, without any trouble and, as
it were, naturally. He acts now not through fear
of hell, but for the love of Christ, out of a good
habit and a delight in virtue.

Once again Benedict demonstrates his belief in
the power of observance or practice. If you do
something often enough, it will become part of
your belief and value system. If you regularly put
other people first and value them and their gifts
before your own, then your attitudes will be
transformed. You will learn to do this 'by habit',
'out of a good habit'. Practice is all.

Chapters on obedience, silence and humility
come at the beginning of the Rule. Benedict's
treatment of the other 'cave-virtues' – poverty
and work – comes later on in the body of the
text. Of the seventy-three chapters, three deal
with poverty (33, 34 and 54) and one with work
(48). Benedict legislates for the common life. 'All
things are to be common to all.' This means that
his teaching on poverty is not about deprivation;

it is about ownership. Everything belongs to everyone, so he says, 'No one, without leave of the abbot, shall presume to give, or receive, or keep as his own, anything whatever: neither book, nor tablets, nor pen: nothing at all.' This is legislation for a learned community; the most precious objects are those which are held in common and shared out among the brethren.

Benedict balances this centralisation with a humane piece of legislation about the needs of individuals. He goes to the Acts of the Apostles for inspiration:

> It is written, 'Distribution was made to everyone, according as he had need'. By this we do not mean that there is to be a personal preference (which God forbid), but a consideration for infirmities. In this wise let him who needs less thank God and be not distressed, and let him who requires more be humiliated because of his infirmity, and not puffed up; by the mercy that is shown him: so all members shall be at peace.

The goal of the common life, the goal of poverty,

is peace between the brethren, and this can best be achieved by a sane, balanced understanding of individuals and their requirements, rather than by blanket legislation which tells people what they may or may not have. There is no sense of threat here. Benedict is anxious to provide generously for his monks and to know each of them well enough to provide for their needs. Benedictine poverty becomes a humanising influence; no wonder Abbot Gasquet noted the Rule's role in civilising Europe.

When he reflects on work, Benedict writes, 'Idleness is the enemy of the soul ... Because this is so the brethren ought to be occupied at specified times in manual labour, and at other fixed hours to holy reading ... They are truly monks when they live by the labour of their hands, as our Father and the Apostles did. Let everything, however, be done with moderation for the sake of the faint-hearted.' Benedict is not interested in sprinters, in those who can shine for a brief moment but then get burnt out. Good habits can only be practised within time, so the use of time must be moderated. Staying power, fidelity to the monastic vocation with its central call of obedience, is all.

Benedict's chapter on 'daily manual labour' is remarkable because it tells the monks that they should spend time reading. Scholarship is an integral part of the Benedictine tradition. Reading the Scriptures or Church Fathers is a way of praying. The tradition calls it *lectio divina* and commends the slow reading of a sacred text in order to illuminate and warm the human heart. So Benedict writes, 'Let the brethren be occupied in reading.' There is even a Sabbath rule:

> On Sunday also, all, save those who are assigned to various offices, shall have time for reading. If, however, anyone be so negligent and slothful as to be unwilling or unable to read or meditate, he must have some work given him, so as not to be idle. For weak brethren, or those of delicate constitutions, some work or craft shall be found to keep them from idleness, and yet not such as to crush them by the heavy labour or to drive them away. The weakness of such brethren must be taken into consideration by the abbot.

Reading is not an alternative, a luxury; it is a requirement. If anything, other kinds of work are the alternative, a substitution for the discipline of scholarship, the discipline of meditation and prayer. Reading feeds the soul; it offers the mind fresh ideas. In a silent community, it provides the challenge of a different opinion; it opens one to God. How wise, then, to have the sentence which reminds us that at times of incapacity or ill health, the abbot must remember the 'weakness of brethren' who cannot cope. All is ordered within time, to meet the dispositions of people as they are, within the events and seasons of everyday life.

The Divine Office

How is time to be measured in the monastery? What are the laws which govern its passing and its observance? The monastic day is a day of prayer; it takes place within liturgical time, time laid out in the seasons of the Church's year. Easter is the high point, with Lent – offering preparation for the true celebration of the Paschal mysteries – as a pivotal moment. Easter corresponds with the coming of summer, so there is an overlay. Nature and grace speak to each other. There are two cycles to the year: the summer period from Easter to 1 November, and the winter season which runs from November on to Easter. As the sun rises for an early dawn, the monk is turned to the source of his true desire, the Son who will rise from the dead. In winter as the light fails, Benedict trims back the observance of liturgical prayer, matching the day to the cycle of available light. Instead of three readings for the evening prayers, there is to be a single reading from the Old Testament, which is to be recited by heart. The backdrop to this legislation is the cycle of light and dark experienced on Monte Cassino; its patterns are those of Campagna.

Benedict wanted the way of life in his monastery to help people be good, not to punish them. 'Nothing harsh or burdensome will be ordained,' he had written in his Prologue. That is why every monk was to have his own bed and his own bedclothes, even though they shared a common dormitory. Of the moment of wakening, the moment when winter erupts into summer – with no gentle spring to herald its arrival – he wrote, 'When they rise for the Divine Office let them gently encourage one another, because of the excuses made by those that are drowsy.'

Each week has its own rhythms, too, built around the celebration of Sunday. This is the day when the cooks change their rotas; in the monastic refectory the readers are changed around as well, marking the beginning of the new week. The monks rise early and begin the day with renewed prayer. On Sunday, as on every other day, Benedict's teaching carries its full force: 'The prophet says, "Seven times I have sung thy praises". This sacred number of seven will be kept by us if we perform the duties of our service in the Hours of Lauds, Primes, Tierce, Sext, None, Evensong and Compline. At these times, therefore, let us give praise to our Creator for his just judgements.' A praying monk prays for the Church as well as for himself. That is why the discipline of the Daily Office is set out in such detail in the Rule. The monk does not pray when he feels like it; he prays when the community prays.

Throughout the year, the monastic hours invite the monk to pray with the psalms. The Christian community has used the Bible as a source book for prayer since its earliest days. The prayer life of the Church has been sustained for centuries by the daily recitation of psalms and canticles from the Hebrew and Christian traditions. Thomas Merton, the Cistercian monk, noted that it was only after about seven years in his monastery, only after seven years of praying the psalms daily, that he began to understand what they were about. Their rhythms had become the rhythms around which he built his days; their metaphors had become the figures of speech in his own thinking and feeling; their words had become his catchphrases. The psalms give us privileged access into what it means to pray. No wonder their rhythms, metaphors and words inspired Jesus in his ministry.

Opus Dei

What is the ministry of the monks? What work do they do in God's service? Their primary work is prayer, which means the Divine Office as well as personal prayer through the slow meditative reading of the Scriptures, or conversation with God in the silence of one's heart. But no one can pray all day long and there is other work to be done. The monk vows obedience to his abbot and the abbot requires of him that he take his turn in performing the tasks of monastic life – taking care of the garden, the library, or the abbey church or kitchen. 'Whenever you begin to do anything,' says Benedict, 'say a prayer.' This prayer underscores the insight that to work is to pray. Without work, there can be no true religious life.

The Gospels themselves teach us this: 'Jesus said to his disciples, "My food is to do the will of him who sent me and to complete his work. Do you not say, 'Four months more, then comes the harvest'? But I tell you, look around you, and see how the fields are ripe for harvesting. The reaper is already receiving wages and is gathering fruit for eternal life, so that sower and reaper may rejoice together"' (John 4:34–6). This example from agriculture is a powerful reminder that work does not go away. A field is more than a beautiful view; it is a task. Moreover the sower is also the harvester and the one who has prepared the ground by ploughing it. At the end of his life, Jesus again speaks of achieving his task; he has completed his work. 'I glorified you on earth by finishing the work that you gave me to do' (John 17:4). The good servant in a Gospel parable is the one who labours away even when his master is not present, and who then reaps a reward.

The divine task which Jesus undertook when he was born was the redemption of souls. The praying, labouring monk shares in the redemptive work which Jesus began. If we work as a prayer, as part of a discipline of love, we do so in the way Benedict intended. Is that why he was so concerned about the tools with which the monks work? The abbot is to appoint monks 'to keep the iron tools, the clothes, or other property of the monastery'. They have power over their fellow monks, so we read: 'If anyone shall treat the property of the monastery in a slovenly or careless way, let him be corrected.' The work of love cannot be pursued with broken tools. Nor can broken men work with any conviction, and Benedict's rules for the treatment of those with infirmities display an edifying concern for emotional as well as physical health.

The truly sick are a special charge of the abbot. 'But let the sick themselves bear in mind that they are served for the honour of God, and should not grieve their brethren who serve them by their superfluous demands.' They are given a separate cell, 'an attendant who is God-fearing, diligent and painstaking', as well as baths and a special allowance of meat to improve their condition. From these small beginnings spring the monastic legacy of herb gardens, natural cures and a wealth of pharmaceutical knowledge. For much medical knowledge was gathered in the monasteries, long before any public provision was made for the care of the sick. Amongst the visitors to any medieval monastery were always those who came to see the infirmarian.

Benedict's legislation about the kitchen comes before his thinking about food and how much or how little the monks should eat. In the kitchen, charity should prevail: 'The brethren are so to serve each other that no one be excused from the work of the kitchen unless on the score of health, or because he is occupied in some matter of great utility, for then great reward is obtained and charity is exercised.' Working in the kitchen is a call to humility and a call to love. The text is curiously detailed. We are told that there is a weekly rota and that before handing on responsibility at the end of his period of service, the outgoing monk must clean up everything. Lest we see this as an early form of kitchen hygiene, the Rule goes on to add a bit of local colour that reminds us that Benedict's world was different from our own. 'He must wash the towels with which the brethren wipe their hands and feet.'

When it comes to food, Benedict fulfils his own command, for he had said that he wanted to impose 'nothing harsh or burdensome'. An undefined amount of wine was allowed each day. The quantity is usually translated as a pint, but we have no method for knowing what that means, nor its strength. With this goes the staple of a pound weight of bread and two dishes of cooked food and one of fruit or vegetables. More significantly, Benedict notes that the abbot may adjust the quantities if there is heavy work to be done. For the monks are not to go in need: 'Dinner at the sixth hour shall be the rule at the discretion of the abbot, if they have work in the fields, or the heat of the summer be great. Let the abbot so temper and arrange everything that souls may be saved, and that what the brethren do may be done without just complaint.' This is practical wisdom, aimed at the care of souls as well as bodies.

So too with the allocation of clothes and bedding. At a time when most labourers would have been hard put to own more than a blanket, Benedict decreed that every monk should have 'a mattress, blanket, coverlet and pillow'. Each will also have 'a cowl, tunic, shoes, stockings, girdle, knife, pen, needle, handkerchief and tablets'. In the detail of Benedict's text, we are shown a snapshot of life at Monte Cassino. The tableau of monastic life is suddenly animated as we see a monk reach for his knife to sharpen his pen and settle down to work on his tablet, or sit down with his needle to mend a frayed cowl.

Yet whatever the detail, Benedict's real legacy is the spirit of the Rule. The warm heart of the document is the man who stands at its very centre, the abbot, the man whose charge is to model the life of Christ and who is helped inestimably in his task by contemplating the story of Benedict, the most extraordinary monk of all time.

Eternal God, who made Benedict to
    become a wise master
in the school of your service
and a guide to many called into community
to follow the rule of Christ:
grant that we may put your love before all else
and seek with joy
the way of your commandments;
through Jesus Christ our Lord,
who is alive and reigns with you,
in the unity of the Holy Spirit,
One God, now and for ever, Amen.

The Christian Year

PART THREE

The Rule

PART THREE

———◆———

The Rule

These selected readings from the Rule of Benedict offer a further insight into its true character, as well as opening the mind of Benedict to us. The translation is by Abbot Gasquet, and dates from 1909.

What the abbot should be (Chapter 2)
An abbot to be fit to rule a monastery should ever remember what he is called, and in his acts illustrate his high calling. For in a monastery he is considered to take the place of Christ, since he is called by his name as the apostle saith, 'Ye shall receive the spirit of adoption of sons, whereby we cry Abba, Father.' Therefore the abbot should neither teach, ordain, nor require anything against the command of our Lord (God forbid!), but in the minds of his disciples let his orders and teaching be mingled with the leaven of divine justice.

The abbot should ever be mindful that at the dread judgement of God there will be inquiry both as to his teaching and as to the obedience of his disciples. Let the abbot know that any lack of goodness will be accounted the shepherd's fault. On the other hand, he shall be acquitted in so far as he shall have shown all the watchfulness of a shepherd over a restless and disobedient flock: and if as their pastor he shall have employed every care to cure their corrupt manners, he shall be declared guiltless in the Lord's judgement.

The abbot in his teaching should always observe that apostolic rule which saith, 'reprove, entreat, rebuke' (2 Tim. 4:2). That is to say, as occasions require he ought to mingle encouragement with reproofs. Let him manifest the sternness of a master and the loving affection of a father. He must reprove the undisciplined and restless severely, but he should exhort such as are obedient, quiet and patient, for their better profit.

The abbot ought ever to bear in mind what he is and what he is called; he ought to know that to whom more is entrusted, from him more is exacted. Let him recognise how difficult and how hard a task he has undertaken, to rule souls and to make himself a servant to the humours of many. One, forsooth, must be led by gentle words, another by sharp reprehension, another by persuasion; and thus shall he so shape and adapt himself to the character and intelligence of each, that he not only suffer no loss in the flock entrusted to his care, but may even rejoice in its good growth. Above all things let him not slight nor make little of the souls committed to his care, heeding more fleeting, worldly and frivolous things; but let him remember always that he has undertaken the government of souls, of which he shall also have to give an account.

On taking counsel of the brethren (Chapter 3)
Whenever any weighty matters have to be transacted in the monastery let the abbot call together all the community and himself propose the matter for discussion. After hearing the advice of the brethren let him consider it in his own mind, and then do what he shall judge most expedient. We

ordain that all must be called to council, because the Lord often reveals to a younger member what is best. And let the brethren give their advice with all humble subjection, and presume not stiffly to their own opinion. Let them rather leave the matter to the abbot's discretion, so that all submit to what he shall deem best. As it becometh disciples to obey their master, so doth it behove the master to dispose of all things with forethought and justice.

In all things, therefore, everyone shall follow the Rule as their master, and let no one rashly depart from it. In the monastery no one is to be led by the desires of his own heart, neither shall any one within or without the monastery presume to argue wantonly with the abbot. If he presume to do so let him be subjected to punishment according to the Rule.

The abbot himself, however, must himself do all things in the fear of God and according to the Rule, knowing that he shall undoubtedly have to give an account of his whole government to God, the most just judge.

If anything of less moment has to be done in

the monastery let the abbot take advice of the seniors only, as it is written, 'Do all things with counsel, and thou shalt not afterwards repent of it.'

The instruments of good works (Chapter 4)
First of all, to love the Lord God with all our heart, with all our soul, with all our strength.

2. Then, to love our neighbour as ourself.
3. Then, not to kill.
4. Not to commit adultery.
5. Not to steal.
6. Not to be covetous.
7. Not to bear false witness.
8. To respect all men.
9. Not to do to another what one would not have done to oneself.
10. To deny oneself in order to follow Christ.
11. To chastise the body.
12. Not to be fond of pleasures.
13. To love fasting.
14. To give refreshment to the poor.
15. To clothe the naked.
16. To visit the sick.

17. To bury the dead.

18. To come to the help of those in trouble.

19. To comfort those in sadness.

20. To become a stranger to the ways of the world.

21. To prefer nothing to the love of Christ.

22. Not to give way to wrath.

23. Not to harbour anger for any time.

24. Not to foster deceit in the heart.

25. Not to make a false peace.

26 Not to depart from charity.

27. Not to swear at all, lest one forswears.

28. To speak the truth with heart and lips.

29. Not to return evil for evil.

30. Not to do an injury, but patiently to suffer one when done.

31. To love one's enemies.

32. Not to speak ill of those who speak ill of one, but rather to speak well of them.

33. To suffer persecution for justice sake.

34. Not to be proud.

35. Not to be a winebibber.

36. Not to be a great eater.

37. Not to be given to sleep.

38. Not to be slothful.

39. Not to be a murmurer.

40. Not to be a detractor.

41. To put one's trust in God.

42. When one sees any good in oneself to attribute it to God, not to oneself.

43. That a man recognise that it is he who does evil, and so let him attribute it to himself.

44. To fear the day of judgement.

45. To be afraid of hell.

46. To desire life everlasting with entire spiritual longing.

47. To have the vision of death before one's eyes daily.

48. To watch over the actions of one's life every hour of the day.

49. To know for certain that God sees one everywhere.

50. To dash at once against Christ (as against a rock) evil thoughts which rise up in the mind.

51. And to reveal all such to one's spiritual Father.

52. To guard one's lips from uttering evil or wicked words.

53. Not to be fond of much talking.
54. Not to speak idle words, or such as move to laughter.
55. Not to love much or boisterous laughter.
56. Willingly to hear holy reading.
57. Often to devote oneself to prayer.
58. Daily with tears and sighs to confess to God in prayer one's past offences, and to avoid them for the future.
59. Not to give way to the desires of the flesh: and to hate one's own will.
60. In all things to obey the abbot's commands, even though he himself (which God forbid) should act otherwise, remembering our Lord's precept, 'What they say, do ye, but what they do, do ye not.'
61. Not to wish to be called holy before one is so; but to be holy first so as to be called such with truth.
62. Daily in one's acts to keep God's commandments.
63. To love chastity.
64. To hate no man.
65. Not to be jealous or envious.

66. Not to love wrangling.
67. To show no arrogant spirit.
68. To reverence the old.
69. To love the young.
70. To love enemies for the love of Christ.
71. To make peace with an adversary before the sun sets.
72. And, never to despair of God's mercy.

Behold these are the tools of our spiritual craft; when we shall have made use of them constantly day and night, and shall have proved them at the day of judgement, that reward shall be given us by our Lord, which he has promised, 'Which every eye hath not seen, nor ear heard, nor hath it entered into the heart of man to conceive what God hath prepared for those that love him' (1 Cor. 2:9). Steadfastly abiding in the community, the workshop where all these instruments are made use of is the cloister of the monastery.

Of the manner of singing in the Office (Chapter 19)
We believe that the Divine Presence is everywhere, and that the eyes of the Lord behold both

the good and the bad in all places. Especially do we believe without any doubt that this is so when we assist at the Divine Office. Let us therefore always be mindful of what the prophet says, 'Serve ye the Lord in fear' (Ps. 2:11); and again, 'Sing ye His praises with understanding' (Ps. 66:8) and 'In the sight of angels I will sing praise to Thee' (Ps. 137:1). Wherefore let us consider how it behoveth to be in the sight of God and the angels, and so let us take our part in the psalmody that mind and voice accord together.

On reverence at prayer (Chapter 20)

If, when we wish to obtain some favour from those who have the power to help us, we dare not ask except with humility and reverence, how much more reason is there that we should present our petitions to our Lord God of the universe in all lowliness of heart and purity of devotion. We may know for certain that we shall be heard, not because we use many words, but on account of the purity of our hearts and our tears of sorrow. Our prayer, therefore, should be short and pure, unless by some inspiration of divine grace it be prolonged. All prayer made by the community in common, however, should be short; and when the prior (that is, the superior) has given the sign, let all rise together.

How the monks are to sleep (Chapter 22)

All shall sleep in separate beds and each shall receive, according to the appointment of his abbot, bedclothes, fitting to the condition of his life. If it be possible let them all sleep in the common dormitory, but if their great number will not allow this they may sleep in tens or twenties, with seniors to have charge of them. Let a candle be constantly burning in the room until morning, and let the monks sleep clothed and girt with girdles or cords; but they are not to have knives by their sides in their beds, lest perchance they be injured whilst sleeping. In this way the monks shall always be ready to rise quickly when the signal is given and hasten each one to come before his brother to the Divine Office, and yet with all gravity and modesty.

What care the abbot should have of the excommunicated (Chapter 27)

The abbot ought to have the greatest care and to use all prudence and industry to love the sheep entrusted to him. Let him know that he hath undertaken the care of souls that are sick, and not act the tyrant over such as are well. Let him fear the reproach of the prophet in which God speaks thus, 'What ye saw to be fat that ye took to yourselves, and what was diseased ye threw away' (Ezek. 34:3). Let him copy the example of the Good Shepherd, who, leaving the ninety-nine sheep in the mountains, went to seek the one that had gone astray, and on whose infirmity he took such compassion that he deigned to lay it on his shoulders and carry it back to the flock.

What manner of man the cellarer of the monastery ought to be (Chapter 31)

Let one of the community be chosen as cellarer of the monastery, who is wise, mature in character, temperate, not a great eater, not arrogant nor quarrelsome, nor insolent, and not a dawdler, nor wasteful, but one who fears God and is as a

Father to the community. Let him have the charge of everything; do nothing without the abbot's order; see to what is commanded, and not make the brethren sad. If any of them shall perchance ask something unreasonable he must not vex him by contemptuously rejecting his request, but humbly and reasonably refuse what he wrongly asks.

Let him look after his own soul, mindful of the Apostolic principle, that 'they that ministered well, shall purchase to themselves a good degree' (1 Tim. 3:13). Let him take every care of the sick, of children, of guests, and of the poor, knowing that he shall have to render an account of all these on the judgement day.

Let him look upon all the vessels and good of the monastery as if they were the consecrated chalices of the altar. He must not think anything can be neglected; he must not be covetous, nor a prodigal wasting the goods of the monastery; but let him do everything with forethought and according to the direction of his abbot.

And above all things let him have humility

and give a gentle answer to those to whom he can give nothing else, for it is written, 'A good word is above the best gift' (Eccl. 18:17). Let him take charge of all the abbot shall commit to him, but let him not meddle with anything which is forbidden him. Let him provide the brethren with their appointed allowance of food without impatience or delay, so that they be not driven to offend, being mindful of the divine word which declares the punishment he deserves, 'Who shall scandalise one of these little ones. It were better for him that a millstone should be hanged about his neck, and that he should be drowned in the depth of the sea' (Matt. 18:6). If the community be large let him be given helpers, by whose aid he may without worry perform the office committed to him. What is given let it be given, and what is asked for let it be asked at suitable times, so that no one be troubled or distressed in the House of God.

Of the sick brethren (Chapter 36)
Before all things and above all things special care must be taken of the sick, so that in very deed

they be looked after as if it were Christ himself who was served. He himself has said, 'I was sick and ye visited me; and what ye did to one of these, my least brethren, ye did to me' (Matt. 18:6). But let the sick themselves bear in mind that they are served for the honour of God, and should not grieve their brethren who serve them by their superfluous demands. These, nevertheless, must be borne with patience, since from such a more abundant reward is obtained. Let the abbot, therefore, take the greatest care that the sick suffer no neglect.

For them let a separate cell be set apart with an attendant who is God-fearing, diligent and painstaking. Let baths be granted to the sick as often as it shall be expedient, but to those in health, and especially to the young, they shall be seldom permitted. Also for the recovery of their strength the use of meat may be allowed to the sick and those of very weak health. As soon, however, as they shall mend they must all in the accustomed manner abstain from flesh meat. Let the abbot take special care that the sick be not neglected by the cellarer or the attendants, because he is responsible for what is done amiss by his disciples.

Concerning old men and children (Chapter 37)
Although human nature itself inclines us to show pity and consideration to age, to the old, that is, and to children, still it is proper that the authority of the Rule should provide for them. Let their weakness be always taken into account, and let the full rigour of the Rule as regards food be in no ways maintained in their regard. There is to be a kind consideration for them and permission is to be given them to anticipate the regular hours.

Of the amount of food (Chapter 39)
We believe that it is enough to satisfy just requirement if in the daily meals, at both the sixth and ninth hours, there be at all seasons of the year two cooked dishes, so that he who cannot eat of the one may make his meal of the other. Therefore two dishes of cooked food must suffice to all the brethren, and if there be any fruit or young vegetables these may be added to the meal as a third dish. Let a pound weight of

bread suffice for each day, whether there be one meal or two, that is, for dinner and supper. If there is to be supper a third of a pound is to be kept back by the cellarer and given to the brethren at that meal.

If, however, the community has been occupied in any great labour it shall be at the will, and in the power of the abbot, if he think fit, to increase the allowance, so long as every care be taken to guard against excess, and that no monk be incapacitated by surfeiting. For nothing is more contrary to the Christian spirit than gluttony, as our Lord declares, 'Take heed to yourselves lest perhaps your hearts be overcharged with surfeiting' (Luke 21:34). And the same quantity shall not be given to young children, but a lesser amount to those older; frugality being maintained in everything. All, save the very weak and sick, are to abstain wholly from eating the flesh of quadrupeds.

Of the measure of drink (Chapter 40)
'Every one hath his proper gift from God, one thus, another thus' (1 Cor. 7:7). For this reason

the amount of other people's food cannot be determined without some misgiving. Still, having regard to the weak state of the sick, we think that a pint of wine a day is sufficient for any one. But let those to whom God gives the gift of abstinence know that they shall receive their proper reward. If either local circumstances, the amount of labour, or the heat of summer require more, it can be allowed at the will of the prior, care being taken in all things that gluttony creep not in.

Although we read that 'wine is not the drink of monks at all,' yet, since in our days they cannot be persuaded of this, let them at least agree not to drink to satiety, but sparingly, 'Because wine maketh even the wise to fall away' (Eccl. 19:2).

That the brethren be obedient to each other (Chapter 71)

The excellent virtue of obedience is to be shown by all, not to the abbot only, but to brethren who shall also mutually obey each other, knowing that by this path of obedience they shall go to

God. The commands of the abbot, or of other superiors constituted by him, having the first place (for to these we do not allow any private orders to be preferred) the juniors shall obey their seniors with all charity and diligence. If any one be found contentious let him be punished.

If a brother be rebuked for even the least thing by the abbot, or by any prior, or if he shall perceive that the mind of any superior is, however slightly, moved against him, or in anger with him, let him without delay prostrate himself at his feet, and remain offering satisfaction until the feeling be removed and he receive a blessing. If any one be found too proud to do this let him be expelled from the monastery.

Of the good zeal monks should have (Chapter 72)
As there is an evil and bitter emulation which separates from God and leads to hell, so there is a good spirit of emulation which frees from vices and leads to God and life everlasting. Let monks therefore practise this emulation with most fervent love; that is to say, let them 'in honour prevent one another', let them bear most patiently

with each other's infirmities, whether of body or of manner. Let them contend with one another in their obedience. Let no one follow what he thinks most profitable to himself, but rather what is best for another. Let them show brotherly charity with a chaste love. Let them fear God and love their abbot with sincere and humble affection, and set nothing whatever before Christ, who can bring us unto everlasting life.

That all perfection is not contained in this Rule (Chapter 73)

We have written this Rule, that, by its observance in monasteries, we may show that we have in some measure uprightness of manners or the beginning of religious life. But for such as hasten onward to the perfection of holy life there are the teachings of the Holy Fathers, the observance whereof leads a man to the heights of perfection. For what page or what passage of the divinely inspired books of the Old and the New Testament is not a most perfect rule for man's life? Or what book is there of the Holy Catholic Fathers that doth not proclaim this, that by a direct course we may come to our Creator? Also, what else are the Collations of the Fathers, their Institutes, their Lives, and the Rule of our Holy Father St Basil, but examples of the virtues, or the good living and obedience of monks? But to us who are slothful, and lead bad and negligent lives, they are matter for shame and confusion.

Do thou therefore, whosoever thou art who hasteneth forward to the heavenly country, accomplish first, by the help of Christ, this little Rule written for beginners, and then at length shalt thou come, under God's guidance, to the lofty heights of doctrine and virtue, which we have spoken of above.

FURTHER READING

FURTHER READING

Byrne, Lavinia, *Sharing the Vision*, SPCK, 1989

Cabrol, Fernand, OSB, *Saint Benedict*, Burns, Oates and Washbourne Ltd, 1934

Clement, Olivier, *The Roots of Christian Mysticism*, New City, 1993

Gasquet, Abbot (trans.), *The Rule of Saint Benedict*, Chatto and Windus, 1909

Gregory the Great, St, *The Life and Miracles of St Benedict*, Liturgical Press, Minnesota, 1948

Louth, Andrew, *The Origins of the Christian Mystical Tradition*, Oxford University Press, 1981 von Matt, Leonard, and Hilpisch, Dom Stephan, OSB, *Saint Benedict*, Burns and Oates, 1961

Parry, David, *The Household of God*, Darton, Longman & Todd, 1980

'Spiritual Direction in the Benedictine Tradition' (Traditions of Spiritual Guidance), The Way, vol 27, no 1, January 1987

de Waal, Esther, *A Life Giving Way*, Geoffrey Chapman, 1995

de Waal, Esther, *Seeking God*, Collins Fount, 1984

Saints for Young Christians

DAVID PREVITALI

Eighty-three fascinating stories relating the lives and experiences of nearly 100 saints are told here in an entertaining, catechetical fashion. Each emphasizes the way in which that particular saint lived the Good News of Jesus in his or her own life. The illustrations enhance the narrative and make it easier for the reader to identify and relate to the saint whose life and works are under discussion. Young people, parents and teachers alike will warm to the solid and yet devotional way in which this work makes the lives of the saints come alive.

Saints Gabriel Possenti, Passionist

GABRIEL CINGOLANI, C.P.

Falling in love is a fundamental event of life. It means not only getting the boy or the girl of one's dreams, but above all finding a reason for living life passionately. Francis Possenti of Assisi, who became Gabriel of Our Lady of Sorrows as a Passionist, fell in love with a girl, as was normal for an 18-year-old boy. But when he realized that there was also another way to fulfill himself in an overflowing of love: by spending his life for God and others. He gave himself so completely that at 24, his life had been used up. This is his story.

Thérèse of Lisieux and
Marie of the Trinity

PIERRE DESCOUVEMONT

Marie-Louis Castel was 20 years old when she entered the Carmel of Lisieux in 1894 and became the novice of St. Thérèse of the Child Jesus. For the next 50 years she put into practice in her daily life the "little way" taught to her by her saintly novice mistress. Suffering terribly from a painful facial ulcer in the final years of her life, she remained always faithful to "the spirituality of the smile." Her favorite saying which she had learned from St. Thérèse and which she was known often to repeat was, "No! Life is not sad!" It's an attitude and outlook on life that is found on every page of this inspiring work.